P9-APE-413

HARVEY PEKAR'S CLEVELAND

Co-Published by:

Zip Comics
237 Griffen Avenue
Scarsdale, NY 10583

Top Shelf Productions
PO Box 1282
Marietta, GA 30061-1282

First Printing, February 2012. Printed in China.

www.topshelfcomix.com
www.zipcomic.com

ISBN: 978-1-60309-091-9

1. Autobiography/Harvey Pekar
2. History/Cleveland, Ohio
3. Graphic Novels

Cover design by Joseph Remnant and Chris Ross
Book design by Chris Ross

Dedicated to:

Danielle from Harvey
&
Hilary from Joseph

Introduction
by Alan Moore

"Yeah, I've had plenty of good days." Thus commences one of the very last and one of the very greatest works by that unique and irreplaceable American voice, the truly splendorous Harvey Pekar. It's a typically generous statement from a man never famous for his cheerfulness, an opening line that takes all the bad days as read and is eager to move along and talk about the good ones, talk about the beloved stuff, talk about Cleveland.

Harvey Pekar was and is one of the very finest writers ever to grace the comic medium, a fact frequently overlooked, perhaps as a result of Harvey the gigantic character overshadowing Harvey the fiercely original and accomplished author in his audience's imagination. Never trafficking in fiction, his work studiously avoids narrative flash and the twist-ending storytelling gimmickry that tends to draw attention to the writer rather than to what his or her writing is about. By way of a result, this sometimes means that much of the sheer craft and ingenuity ofHarvey's output goes unnoticed by a readership who are not preconditioned to expect or notice subtlety.

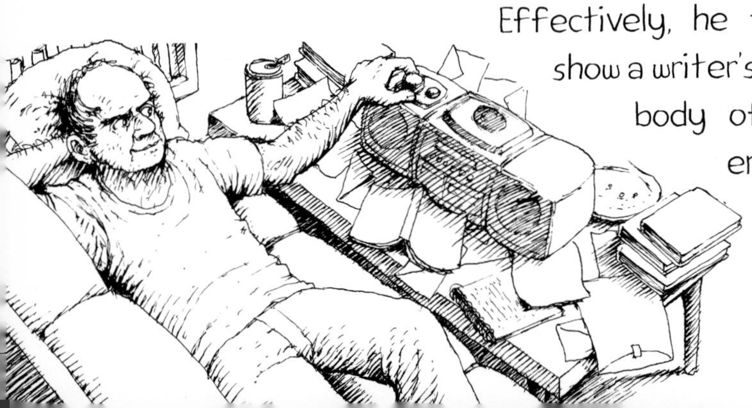

Effectively, he takes care not to show a writer's hand in his immense body of work, placing the emphasis on his exquisite eye and ear. This is where his genius resides: not in elaborate contrivance of baroque adventures, but in simply witnessing the marvellous abundance of astonishing phenomena surrounding him in his plain, ordinary human life. Whether the musicality of a co-worker's chance remark or lyric quality to some mundane transaction, Harvey notices it and then writes it down so everyone can share his fugitive perceptions. Generally impoverished, his world is nevertheless rich in observation to the point where fiction is unnecessary; to the point where making something up is practically an insult to the stunning bounty of prosaic existence. Every panel celebrates the worth of being who we are, and when we are, and where we are; the value of our individual lives and times, and of the shabby, legendary places where we live.

In Harvey's case, that would be Cleveland. Accurately, he treats human dramas, triumphs and turmoils as emergent properties of landscape, just as he conversely treats the streets and towns around us as extensions of ourselves. A person or a place cannot be fully understood unless each is considered in the context of the other. Cleveland is a part of Harvey Pekar, just as in his resting place amongst the like of John D. Rockefeller, Elliot Ness and various illustrious untouchables him and his story are eternally part of the narrative of Cleveland, with the man and his environment inseparably become one thing. *Harvey Pekar's Cleveland* is to my mind the most beautiful expression of that intricate and intimate relationship, a eulogy for a lost city and, increasingly, for a lost social class.

Lucidly weaving his hometown's revealingly average geopolitical history with that of his immigrant family and background, characteristically non-judgemental, Harvey gives us what will almost certainly come to be seen as an essential American document. As a last work, encapsulating everything that Harvey Pekar and his writing are about and delivered at the absolute peak of his form, it is the perfect celebratory firework display, the best note that he could conceivably go out on. Furthermore, in an unusually benevolent and welcome quirk of fortune, this final and arguably finest offering is graced by the impeccable and poignant artistry of Joseph Remnant, in my opinion perhaps the most sensitively-tuned collaborator on Harvey's already-stellar roster. The exhaustively researched depictions of a vanished world and haunting evocations of its atmosphere provide an ideal complement to the warm rasp of the authorial tone, a seamless match appropriate to this magnificent, majestic consummation of a dedicated writer's life, career and heartfelt passion for his habitat.

Yeah, he's had plenty of good days, and so has Cleveland. Here between these covers are the sweet and bitter fruits gathered from just a few of them.

Alan Moore
Northampton
(a formerly prosperous town
in the middle of a formerly prosperous country)
August 7th, 2011

Alan Moore is a writer of graphic novels including *Watchmen*, *V for Vendetta*, *League of Extraordinary Gentlemen*, *From Hell*, and *Lost Girls*.

HARVEY PEKAR'S CLEVELAND

WRITTEN BY
HARVEY PEKAR

ILLUSTRATED BY
JOSEPH REMNANT

EDITED BY
JEFF NEWELT

Yeah, I've had plenty of good days...

...but when people ask me which was the best, the first to come to mind is when I was listening to the elementary school PA system as the Cleveland Indians clinched a victory over the Boston Braves (later the Milwaukee Braves and Atlanta Braves) to win the 1948 World Series.

I mean, I'd heard plenty of pro-Cleveland propaganda by the time I'd reached the fourth grade. I thought it was fine that Cleveland had a great symphony orchestr a huge public library, that one of the tallest buildings in the world (the Terminal Tower) was located here, that we had a public park system that was the envy of the country, and that Cleveland was one of the U.S.'s biggest manufacturing center

But to me what mattered was sports – I checked out the record book and found that Cleveland had last won the World Series in 1920 and usually finished in the middle or near the bottom of the American League. Nobody figured they were a World Series competitor. They'd finished fourth in the league in '47.

But this team had some key young players. There was rookie pitcher Gene Bearden, a war hero, who had a 20-7 record.

There was second-year outfielder Dale Mitchell, who hit .335.

And Larry Doby, the first black player in the American League in 1947, who hit .301 in '48.

There was Satchel Paige, the legendary Negro League pitcher. The newspapers made a big deal about his age. Some said he was in his late 30s, some in his 70s.

Paige was 6-1 in 1948, a definite help to the team, not just a curiosity.

STEE-RIKE THREE!

Then, too, there was the dashing player-manager Lou Boudreau. There haven't been many player-managers in sports. An outstanding defensive shortstop, Lou hit a .355, a career season, second only to the great Ted Williams.

The Indians' veterans played at least up to par as well – second baseman Joe Gordon hit .280 and slugged 32 home runs.

Third baseman Kenny Keltner hit .297 with 31 homers.

The Indians finished in a dead heat with the Boston Red Sox for the American League championship. In the play-offs, Cleveland won 8-3, with Boudreau going 4 for 4 with 2 home runs, and Bearden being the winning pitcher.

Winning the World Series was the last piece of the puzzle for me. The Cleveland Browns football team won championship after championship.

There was also a minor league hockey team, The Barons, that were often on top. But a **BASEBALL** championship! I never thought I'd see the day.

I remember the Indians ahead in the series three games to two, and in the final game having a 4-1 lead.

But then the pitching faltered. Nevermind, though, Gene Bearden relieves to save a 4-3 victory. You better believe Cleveland went wild that day. Starting with my fourth grade classroom.

YEEAAAAAH!
SSHHH

And you know what? Bearden never had another good year. He was just heaven-sent for one season!

For the next several seasons, the Indians did well, but never WON anything! I figured it wasn't going to happen again. 1948 was a fluke. But I was just happy to have gone through the season.

But wait! In 1954, the same Indians that had consistently finished behind the Yankees won the American League title!

It was amazing. Some guys had career years. Second baseman Bobby Avila held the lead in batting, and Doby led in home runs.

Bob Avila

The Indians won 111 games that year, breaking the 1927 record of the Yankees with Babe Ruth and Lou Gehrig.

But then Cleveland lost the World Series to the New York Giants four games to none.

The Giants' Willie Mays made a fantastic catch of a 460-foot drive to dead center - which was an impossible distance at 505 feet away - in the first game and killed an Indians rally. After that, they just folded.

For me, the 1954 World Series was a turning point. I always looked at the Indians as an up and-coming team. But now they seemed to me rotten to the core with success. Like all they had to do was throw their gloves on the field and they thought they'd win.

A few years later that's how I viewed Cleveland: rotten. And a few years after that, the city started to decline. So did my luck.

KEYS

The year I got out of high school, 1957, there was a big recession going on. I couldn't find a decent, steady job.

HELP WANTED

Well, Cleveland's been around longer than I have, so let's start at the beginning with the city that's been called "the best location in the nation" and more recently, "the mistake by the lake."

In 1795, the state of Connecticut held the "Western Reserve" tract in which Cleveland was to be located.

Investors in the Connecticut Land Company got together and sent an exploratory party, headed by Moses Cleveland, to assess its potential.

Native Americans living in the area also claimed the Western Reserve, but their position was weakened by the U.S.'s victory over them at The Battle of Fallen Timbers.

Cleveland's group negotiated with the Native Americans and made a treaty with them that seemed satisfactory. The Cleveland faction got much of the Western Reserve, and, in the following years, pushed for and got the rest of it.

Cleveland's party of surveyors actually arrived in the Western Reserve in 1796. He noted...

I believe, as now informed, the Cuyahoga River will be the place for the new settlement.

It must command the greatest communication, either by land or water of any river on the purchase or in any ceded lands from the head of the Mohawk to the western extend, or I am no prophet.

The territory at the junction of the Cuyahoga and Lake Erie did seem like a promising land to build a thriving settlement, but got off to a slow start.

The members of the Connecticut Land Company were not interested in settling in the Western Reserve, but in selling plots of land to others who wanted to move there.

Also, the mouth of the Cuyahoga was a breeding ground for insects and disease. As a result, the population in the Western Reserve grew slowly.

Some of the people who moved to the Western Reserve were interested primaril in trading with the Native Americans, not building a strong community.

This kept settlers who were interested in building a growing town away from the area.
I don't want to be the first or second person to move there.

As a matter of fact, in 1800 trader Lorenzo Carter was the only person considered "living in Cleveland;" the small nearby town of Warren was thought to be more stable.

In 1800, there were 1500 people living in the Western Reserve. In 1810, about 17,000.

The area was settled by people from a variety of areas; there was no preponderance of Connecticut citizens.

Ohio became a state in 1803, and gradually the Western Reserve attracted more settlers.

At first, the movement was slowed by the rough kinds of people living there and the threat of malaria growing in the mouth of the Cuyahoga.

Still, there was movement. In 1811, a local lending library was established by 16 Cleveland families.

Though the area's soil was not high quality, a farming community was establishe
as well as flour, milk, and bread manufacturer

In 1806, two roads were joined that connected Cleveland and Buffalo. Cleveland had a young work force and was considered the Western Reserve's primary manufacturing and commercial area. The city became less isolated and would become even less isolated with the completion of the Ohio and Erie Canal.

A solid local government was founde

Finally, the mouth of the Cuyahoga was cleaned out, making for healthier living and increasing Cleveland's port activity. By 1818, it had been visited by a steamboat and seemed to be on its way to at least local prominence.

The importance of the Ohio and Erie Canal, with its northern terminus at Cleveland, was of huge signifigance in adding to efforts to make it a major port. The canal ended at the Ohio River, which joined the Mississippi, thus allowing a huge amount of North-South trade. Cleveland was connected to New Orleans by water.

In view of Cleveland's obvious promise, it received federal funds to improve its harbor.

The town's growth was hampered somewhat by the Panic of 1837, but by 1840 its population was 7500, and it was the fastest growing community over 1000 in the state.

In 1854, Cleveland and Ohio City, which was located on the West Bank of the Cuyahoga, united to form a single town, thus eliminating some contention between the two.

By 1860, Cleveland was considered a physically attractive city and a growing economic powerhouse.

In 1860, Cleveland's population had grown to 43,000. By 1870, it was 93,000.

CLEVELAND INSURANCE

45% of the population was foreign born, mainly from England, Ireland, and Germany.

Well, O'shea, how d'ya like Cleveland?

800 African-Americans lived in Cleveland under reasonably good conditions. They lived mainly in one area, but the city was not as segregated as it was to become. At least some African-Americans were middle class.

The Civil War accelerated Cleveland's rise as an industrial city. It was ideally located to produce iron and steel, located between the iron fields of Michigan and Minnesota, and the coal centers of Pennsylvania.

It gained in importance as a transportation center. Railroad lines passed through the city, and oil refineries sprang up.

It had an impressive "Millionaire's Row" along Euclid Avenue.

As time went on immigrants from Southern and Eastern Europe increasingly populated the city, where they found plenty of work.

Also moving to Cleveland was John D. Rockefeller, who built a monopoly in Standard Oil.

Rockefeller got into the oil business in 1865, and in fifteen to twenty years had captured 90% of American oil refining.

Oil refining depended on sulfuric acid, and chemist Eugene Grasselli came to Cleveland to manufacture the acid.

European immigrants not only worked as laborers. Some became entrepreneurs, such as Hungarian Theodore Rundtz, who owned a cabinet factory.

Cleveland's black population increased in the latter half of the nineteenth century, but stayed at 1% of the total population. Cleveland remained relatively open to them.

With industrialization came labor unrest and union-building in the 1880s and 90s. This was a difficult transition for the labor force to make, but Cleveland relatively quickly became a union town.

1900-1910 saw further commercial and industrial growth. The decade was highlighted by the four mayoral terms of Tom L. Johnson.

He was called by the famous Progressive journalist Lincoln Steffens:

The best mayor of the best governed city in the United States.

Johnson was a disciple of philosopher Henry George. Before becoming mayor, he was a wealthy businessman and served two terms in the U.S. House of Representatives.

He was often cited as one of the most outstanding Progressive politicians of his day, and was something of an urban socialist.

He worked to gain public ownership of the transit system and municipal light plant, and built an attractive downtown section called The Mall.

Johnson was a champion of youth and built many recreational facilities for Cleveland's young people. He banned "Keep off the grass" signs in public parks.

Another highly-thought-of mayor was Newton Baker (1912-16). He realized Johnson's aim of building a municipal light plant and was involved in the selection of the commission that wrote Cleveland's first home rule amendment to the Ohio Constitution.

Later, Baker served under Woodrow Wilson as Secretary of War.

The World War I years saw good economic times for Cleveland, as it produced items used in the war, and the growth of wealthy suburbs.

Around that time, women were still oppressed. They tried tirelessly to obtain political rights, led by social workers and teachers. Finally they were able to get to vote.

African-American Jane Edna Hunter had an important influence in obtaining apartments for homeless black women. She later founded the Phyllis Wheatley Association.

Despite her work, Hunter was blamed for black women being banned from the YMCA.

The early part of the 1900s saw efforts made to segregate blacks and keep them out of the suburbs. Some whites were threatened as their population increased, largely due to the increasing industrial jobs available in Cleveland.

In 1910, Cleveland's population increased to 560,663, making it one of the largest cities in America.

Cleveland became, by some studies, however, the second most segregated city in America.

Blacks did not tolerate their exclusion from the larger society, which led to a great deal of social unrest, and in the 1960s two full scale riots.

SALS BAR

However, building and beautification continued at a rapid pace. More major structures were built, including the Terminal Tower (one of the nation's tallest buildings), the main public library branch, a public auditorium, and a music hall.

To handle incoming and outgoing visitors, a municipal airport was established.

Locally, a rapid transit system was set up from the wealthy suburb of Shaker Heights to downtown.

Long in the works, a lovely park system that ringed Cleveland was created in 1917.

But the prosperity Cleveland enjoyed under Presidents Harding and Coolidge came to a halt in the Herbert Hoover administration. The Great Depression lasted through the 1930s, despite President Roosevelt's efforts.

The Cleveland area continued to grow, however, reaching over 900,000 in 1930. The suburbs were exploding with people too.

Immigrants continued to pour into the city. In 1920, Jews made up 9% of the city's population.

With a Jewish population of 75,000, Cleveland became a major Jewish center.

Also from Eastern Europe came a large stream of Slavic people.

Partly because of fear or distaste for the latest immigrants, many more prosperous Clevelanders fled to the suburbs, and the city's tax base shrank.

SHAKER HEIGHTS
CITY LIMITS

In the mid-teens, the labor movement was growing. 1917 saw Marxist, socialist mayoral candidate Charles Ruthenberg gain about a third of the vote. After the Bolshevik Revolution, Ruthenberg became Executive Secretary of the Communist Party of America.

In 1919, there was a prolonged left-wing riot led by Ruthenberg. After his death in 1927, his ashes were sent to Moscow and buried in the Kremlin Wall. He and John Reed we the only Americans to receive such treatme

Though there was a population increase in 1930, there were several bad signs for Cleveland. Its percentage of the county (Cuyahoga) population decreased from 88% in 1910 to 75% in 1930. In 1930, Cuyahoga County was the third largest metropolitan area in the nation.

Slums were developing in several parts of town.

Of course the Great Depression hit hard, but in April, before the stock market crash, there were 40,000 unemployed. In January 1930, that number had increased to 100,000.
FREE SOUP
FOR THE UNEMPLOYED
JOE'S DELI

Tax revenue declined; money was needed for the many on welfare.

FDR's New Deal programs helped, and in 1938 Mayor Harold Burton balanced the budget, but serious joblessness continued until the build-up of the Second World War.
LOOKING
FOR WORK
NOT
CHARITY
cold drinks

However, a pre-war accomplishment that made native Clevelanders proud was the building of the huge municipal stadium where the Indians' first appearance brought a crowd of 80,000 spectators.

Also impressive was the Great Lakes Exposition, held in Cleveland in 1936-7. It's the closest thing Cleveland had to a World's Fair.

The boom in the 1940s sparked by the Second World War continued for several years after the war's conclusion.

It attracted black and white people from the South and a number of Puerto Ricans.

All seeking jobs, they changed the city's ethnic makeup. During the decade, the black population increased to 148,000. Many lived in ghetto slums.

At the time, Cleveland was an economic powerhouse. But suburbanites did not pay their share of taxes to the city. This hurt and would continue to hurt.

Its iron and steel mills continued to be fed iron ore from Michigan and Minnesota, and coal from Pennsylvania.

Regarding transportation, buses replaced streetcars, the rapid transit system was extended, and several freeways were built.

But the picture wasn't all bleak. The St. Lawrence Seaway, scheduled to open in 1959, would connect Lake Erie to the Atlantic Ocean, enhancing Cleveland as a port.

Beginning in the mid 1950s, a plethora of low-cost housing projects were built in some of Cleveland's shabbiest areas, but these also became rundown and breeding grounds for crime.

There were also ambitious efforts to rebuild downtown, but Clevelanders maintained their flight to the suburbs, and nothing much changed.

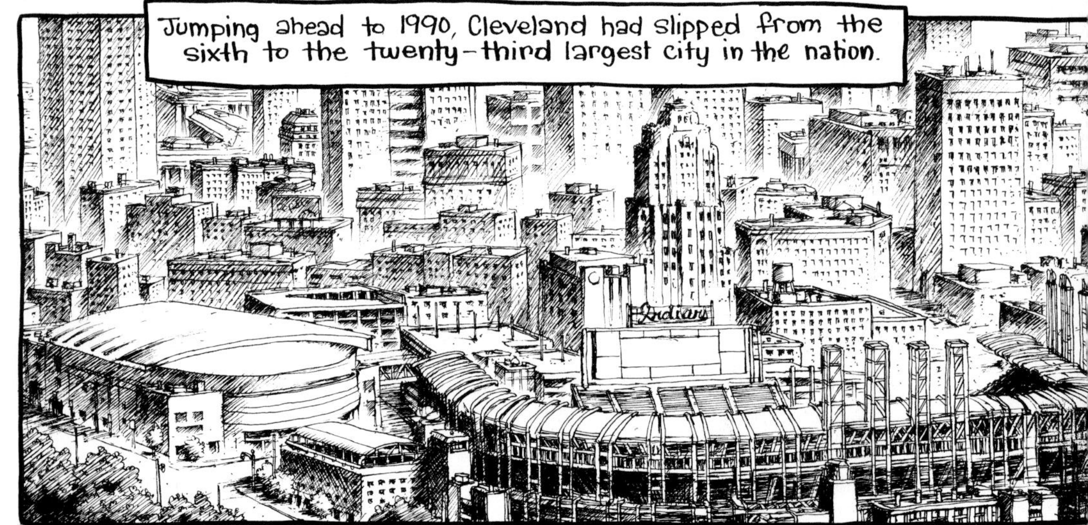
Jumping ahead to 1990, Cleveland had slipped from the sixth to the twenty-third largest city in the nation.

A great deal of public housing was built in the Ghetto; Cleveland was decaying a bit as it grew.

In 1950, Cleveland's population, peaked at 914,000. But crime was increasing. The housing stock decreased in value.

New suburbanites were shopping at suburban shopping centers instead of downtown Cleveland. Industries were settling in the suburbs as well.

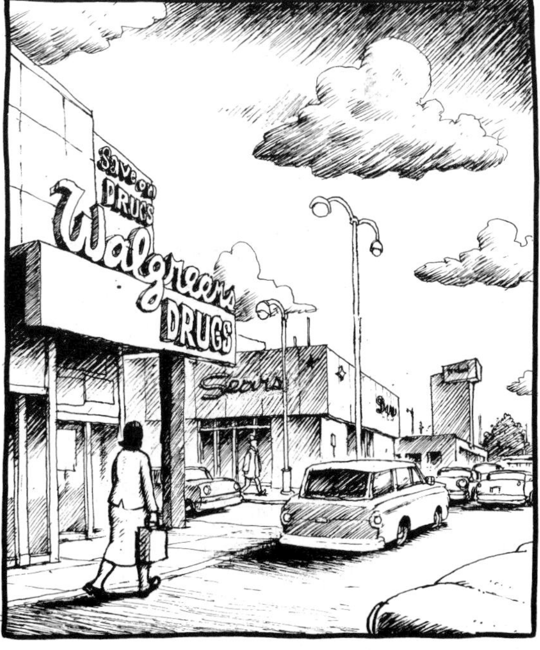
Save-on DRUGS
Walgreens
DRUGS
Sears

The Cleveland economic situation was not helped by competition from other American cities and even foreign nations, where the cost of living was lower. People stopped looking at Cleveland as a source of opportunity. It began to be surpassed economically by southern and southwestern states.

HOUSTON
TEXAS
Memphis
GREETINGS from
PHOENIX
ARIZONA
ATLANTA
Georgia
San Diego
LOUISIANA

Most affected by Cleveland's difficulties was the city's black community. The east side's Hough area had changed from predominantly white to black. 25% of Cleveland's welfare cases were located there by 1964. Street violence was frequent.

Finally, in July 1966, riots broke out in Hough and went on for 4 days.

Vandalism and arson required the National Guard to be called in to restore peace.

This caused a major shock and led to the election of Carl Stokes, the nation's first black mayor, in 1967.

Voters thought the election of Stokes would lead to more racial harmony, but instead, in 1968, riots broke out in Glenville, an area bordering Hough, and again the National Guard was called in.

Its like déjà vu all over again.

Cleveland was now regarded by many whites as an unsatisfactory place to live. Crime-ridden and physically decaying.

Its population had fallen to 573,000 in 1980. The Brookings Institute, in 1975, ranked Cleveland as the second worst big city in the nation, in terms of social and economic problems.

JOBS

From the late 50s to the 70s, retail stores shut down in Cleveland while increasing in the rest of Cuyahoga County.

From 1958 to 1977, the rest of Cuyahoga County surpassed Cleveland in job creation by a huge amount.

WESTLAKE BANK
WESTLAKE BANK & TRUST COMPANY

Also during this time, the Cuyahoga River caught fire, and Mayor Ralph Perk accidentally set his hair on fire. Cleveland's designation as "the mistake by the lake" was heard more often.

However, there were some gains. Downtown was given a boost by the rebuilding of the theatre district (Playhouse Square).

THE LION KING

In the late 70s, there was a serious controversy over the prospect that Cleveland would sell its municipal light plant to a private company (Cleveland was in debt at the time).

Mayor Dennis Kucinich opposed the plan, and a referendum was held. Voters backed Kucinich, and the plant was retained by Cleveland.

However, Kucinich also lost the next election. Once thought of as a boy wonder, he eventually became a U.S. Congressman and a perennial Presidential Candidate.

In 1980, Cleveland began something of a comeback. The size of City Council was reduced to reflect a reduction in population. By cutting a number of city employees and increasing the income tax, the next mayor, George Voinovich, was able to repay Cleveland's debts.

But Cleveland was not, and is not, out of the woods. It has lost a huge number of manufacturing jobs.

UNEMPLOYMENT
CLAIMS

The economy shifted from industrial jobs to lower paying service jobs. Eventually, Cleveland's growing medical facilities became the area's employment leader.

But the city and its older suburban areas continued to decline and become infested with the drug trade.

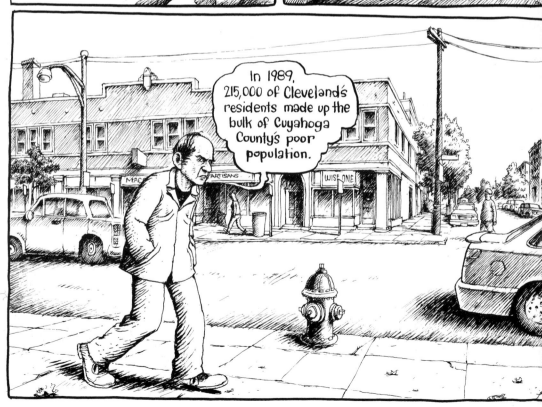

In 1989, 215,000 of Cleveland's residents made up the bulk of Cuyahoga County's poor population.

New clubs appealing to young people appeared, but were patronized by suburban dwellers.

The housing situation was described as the second worst in the nation.

The public school situation was so dire that one superintendent committed suicide.

In 1995, the schools had deteriorated to the point where the State of Ohio was ordered to administer them.

Yes, there were things that some would consider bright spots. New sports venues were built, as was the Rock 'n' Roll Hall of Fame. But again the lot of the average Clevelander, maybe even Cleveland-area residents, had not improved.

What else can be done in Cleveland?! The local transit system has been improved, housing projects have been built, and still Cleveland's economic outlook is bleak! No well-to-do young people want to raise their children here.

Cleveland, THUMBS DOWN!

This is a shame, as Cleveland has more things to recommend it than most cities its size: an outstanding art museum, a world-class orchestra, top notch hospitals, attractive parks, major league sports.

Visitors comment favorably on these, but **REFUSE** to plant **SEEDS** here!
I wouldn't be caught **DEAD** here!

As one who has lived in Cleveland for seventy years, I think the main problem has been race relations.

Perhaps the election of Barack Obama will improve the situation, especially if he is able to solve some of the weighty problems that confront him.
CHAN
WE CAN BELIEV
CHANGE
CHANGE
CHANGE

Admittedly, the situation looks bleak, but, you know...
"Where there's life, there's hope."
1820
MAC'S B CKS BO

I come into the picture in 1939.

Harvey Pekar & Cleveland

I lived on a street where I was the only white kid. For the first few years of my life, I didn't have friends, or acquaintances, for that matter.

Both of my Polish-born parents worked long hours in their mom-and-pop grocery store a few blocks away. I stayed home, sometimes talking Yiddish to my grandfather, who at least had a sense of humor.

Life was pretty grim for my parents. My father was a Talmudic scholar, my mother had an excellent working knowledge of Hebrew and of Jewish religious practices and history.

But until the USSR sided with Egypt instead of Israel in the 1956 Suez crisis, she was an enthusiastic Communist. Above all, though, both were ardent Zionists who wanted Israel to become a nation, which happened in 1948, and for it to survive.

My mother would hear nothing bad about the Communists until they sided with the Egyptians. After that, she had little to say about them.

I used to spend a lot of time on my front porch watching other kids play. They wouldn't accept me. I believed my mother when she told me what hell black people went through just to survive, but did that mean I had to be ostracized? I guess it did.

By that time, racial prejudice had been festering in the USA for far too long. Blacks hung out with blacks, whites with whites, and never did the twain meet.

It was a drag to be sweating, having nothing to do on a hot summer day.

At first, I didn't understand it, but it didn't take me long to realize that race relations were bad.
DINER
WE SERVE WHITES only

During the Second World War, I wondered about what had happened to our Polish relatives. We never heard from them. My parents never spoke about them.

It didn't bother me much at the time. I was a pre-schooler and didn't exactly have a world-view. I'd never met my Polish-Jewish relatives. They were an abstraction to me.

STOP
It was some time later that I learned about the Holocaust.

The Second World War provided plenty of excitement for me. I thought because of the media coverage the outcome would end up with the American side winning. And it did.
CAPTAIN AMERICA

I remember the blackouts, when there'd be a worry about American cities being bombed. Everyone would turn their lights out at night to present a more difficult target for bombers. It was kind of a nuisance for me, since I was so confident of an Allied victory in any event.

At the same time, the total blackness surrounding me was kind of eerie.

When the war was over, and I heard that six million Jews had been murdered, it was beyond my comprehension.
CAR W

Not only my parents, but all my aunts and uncles, as well as some of my cousins, were born in Poland.

My parents worked seven days a week. However, my grandfather, my aunt and uncle, and my three cousins, all 12 to 15 years older than me, gave me attention.

We all lived in the same double house, where everyone spoke Yiddish. My cousin used to kid around with me, nicknaming me CHew-Tongue-Chew and George Wash-The-Floor.

GEORGE WASH-THE-FLOOR!

Because everyone in our double house spoke Yiddish, at one time I could speak it pretty fluently. I lost my ability to speak Yiddish a few years after my grandfather died—he was my most constant Yiddish conversation mate—but I could understand it well for some time after that.

While I was still in elementary school, my parents moved about seventeen blocks up the main drag in the neighborhood to a mostly affluent suburb, Shaker Heights. My parents wanted to expose me to the larger Jewish population there.

I liked my new school and did well in class.

Most of the rest of Shaker Heights consisted of prosperous to posh areas. It was ok, but I never fit in with the richer kids.

I collected comics until I was eleven, when I realized how predictable they were.
Oh man, I know halfway into it how this story's gonna end.
BATMAN

So I switched to kid's novels. I encountered a series of books by Eleanor Estes about the Moffat family, which was being raised by a single mother.

I was amazed at how realistic her writing was. Later, I realized the Moffat series was autobiographical. Looking back on it, I realize Estes was my first literary influence.
Wow, this is so realistic, it's great.

I also was a class clown. I loved to make people laugh.
So this guy sez...

At ten, I started working in my parents' grocery store, thus retaining my connection with African-Americans.
Fresh melons $.

At first, I felt I was really grown up, but pretty soon I became bored with the job, which I held through high school.

During my last year in high school, I also worked as an usher in a neighborhood theatre.

I got interested in sports when I was about eight and enjoyed playing baseball, football, and basketball. I also collected sports magazines and books for a long time. I was always collecting something obsessively.
SPORT

Some nice older neighborhood guys used to take me with them to watch the Cleveland Indians. I got to see more of the city than ever before and was shocked by the slums. The wooden houses looked like they were rotting.

Sometimes I'd go downtown and pick through the books and magazines at Kay's used bookstore, located in a seedy area.

Man, I loved going to Kay's. It was the biggest bookstore I'd ever seen. There was stuff all over the place. I seldom went there without finding some prized item.
Wow, "Football Facts & Figures!" I never saw it outside a library.
FOOTBALL
FACTS AND FIGURES

Kay's used to get hassled by the cops because they carried racy girlie magazines, but I paid no attention to that.

Their shelves were crowded with books of all kinds. I figured if I couldn't find a book there, I couldn't find it anywhere. But I have since run across larger bookstores, even in Cleveland.

In fact, the biggest used bookstore I've ever seen, maybe the biggest in the world, opened decades later. It's owned by a guy named John Zubal on West 25th near Clark. Actually, he bought a big stock of books from Kay's while he was building his empire of the future.
ZONE
2

The store consists of three buildings, with two of them having annexes, one on a former printing plant, the other on a former wholesale florist's. The third huge building used to house the Hostess BaKing Company.

Even now, years after John acquired it, it's possible to eat the Twinkie filling safely. It was all chemicals and didn't deteriorate.

Not bad.

John was about my age and started swapping Tarzan and sci-fi books to Kay's when he was just a bike-riding kid.

We didn't know each other as kids, but he was wheeling and dealing plenty, even then. He'd go all over the West Side (I was from the East Side) looking for books to swap and sell to other bookstores like Nick (the Greek) Pappas' Ace Books, or Pan Books. He also worked for the St. Vincent de Paul stores, emptying houses and picking up hundreds of books in the process.

How much can I get for these?

John, a Ukranian and Byzantine Catholic, went to the mainly Roman Catholic St. Ignatius High School. He was interested in Slavic history, as he is today.

The Hutsuls lived in the Carpathian Mountains. The Lemkovs were Lowlanders.

He's always been what I thought a book dealer should be: learned and able to turn customers on to new stuff.

Back to the past: My neighborhood contained a couple of large parks, and sometimes on Sunday afternoons, when my father closed his store, we'd go to them to attend Jewish affairs.

I loved junk food, and there were plenty of hot dogs, potato chips, and soda pop, so I was in heaven.

In a lot of ways, I wasn't close to my parents. Our backgrounds were dissimilar, and they were always working. But I marveled at how devoted they were to each other. They had so much love and admiration for one another.

Once in a while my parents would take a drive down East Boulevard, or Liberty Boulevard, both of which were located in alley-like spaces, to look at the cultural gardens located on the hills. Just about every ethnic group had a spot there with statues of their heroes, like England might have a statue of one of their kings.

Some had small open buildings. It was a unique and attractive place, not to be found in other cities.

The closest park to us was Woodland Hills; we called it Woodhill Park. It was large and surrounded by Jewish, Hungarian, Italian, and black neighborhoods.

A lot of local league baseball games were played there, from Class F to Class A.

The various teams got along well there. I never heard of any brawls, although at night gangs would congregate in the park and fight with each other.

As I grew older, I learned to use the area's public transit facilities, the electric trolley or street cars, which were later replaced by buses and the rapid transit.

105

The buses were smellier and dirtier than trolleys. Since then, I've learned they were inferior in other ways, and when the environmental movement began, there were a lot of people saying that electric trolleys should have remained the principal mode of public transportation.

When I first saw the center of Cleveland, I was very impressed. There was a very tall building down there called the Terminal Tower.

Its bottom level was a train and rapid transit stop. Anyway, I found, by looking in an old reference book, that for a few months in the 30s, it was the tallest building in the world. Well, better for a short time than never.

Today, there are a couple of buildings in downtown Cleveland that are taller than the Terminal Tower, which no longer seems so tall to me.

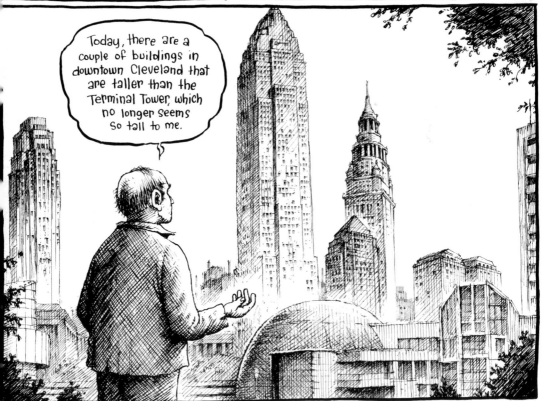

Adjoining the Terminal Tower was Cleveland's largest department store, Higbee's. In its basement was a snack bar where you could get hot dogs, potato chips, Cokes – not very unique stuff.

But they did have one unusual item, a 10-cent chocolate malt that was ice cold. It was called a frosty malt.

Oh, It's so cold it's giving me a headache. It's so thick and creamy!

And man it was good! I guess I hadn't done a lot of malt drinking, just milkshakes. So this chocolate malt thrilled me. If I'd have bought a less good-tasting Pepsi or Coke as large as that, they wouldn't have only charged me 10 cents!

So why were they giving away a treat like this for a DIME!? Maybe it was a loss leader.

Before heading home on the rapid transit, I'd run over to Higbee's for a chocolate malt to fortify myself for my journey.

Another building I liked was the Arcade, which, after a couple of other arcades were built later, became known as the Old Arcade.

It was housed in this big building, six or eight stories high, with both a huge, gold metal staircase (maybe brass) and elevators.

You could go up the steps if you were feeling energetic, or take the elevator.

I'd go to the top of the Arcade, then walk down, looking at all the store windows. They didn't sell stuff I wanted, but it was fun to check out the merchandise.

But a lot of downtown was pretty chintzy. Of course chintzy isn't always bad. I'm kind of a chintzy guy myself.

A buck and a quarter, a buck fifty...

I really dig secondhand thrift stores, and some of the best times I had were going to Kay's.

You never knew what you'd find when you got there.
Wow, I've never seen one a' these.

Mrs. Kay was really nasty to customers, which surprised me. When I met her, she was young and surprisingly pretty, but she had no patience with customers.
C'mon, make up your mind!

You just had to count on getting insulted when you got there.
DON'T HANDLE THOSE MAGAZINES SO ROUGHLY!

I should give her credit for toughening me up in view of some of the troubles I would experience. I learned early that you have to allow for unpleasantness in your life.

Another thing I was into when I was a teenager was pop music.
♫ Why do fools fall in love ♫

This may surprise some people, but Cleveland was a birthplace of hits in the 1950s. We were weeks ahead of Dick Clark.
Is he still playing that old crap?

We had some very effective promoter-DJs in Cleveland. There was this guy from Detroit, Bill Randle, who was especially popular in Cleveland.
WERE

Randle was a particularly interesting case. He could make a hit out of anything. He was far away from a hard core R&B or rock DJ. He promoted Pat Boone—made him a singing star—and he also made corny shit like Mitch Miller's '50s records popular.
AND NOW HERE'S THE **HOT** NEW MITCH MILLER SINGLE!!

All the time Randle was DJing he was going to some graduate school. He had a Ph.D. in American Studies and a law degree.

Actually, Cleveland remains an important pop music center today. Votes from Cleveland fans brought the Rock'n'Roll Hall of Fame to Cleveland.

From pop music I got into jazz, and I mean heavy! I had written for a jazz magazine when I was nineteen.

We had several other notable radio and T.V. hosts. Alan Freed, who introduced R&B to white kids, was very popular in Cleveland before he left for New York.

WABC

He was replaced by Pete (Mad Daddy) Myers, who jumped out of airplanes.

On T.V. we had the satirical Ghoulardi (Ernie Anderson), who started a trend by dressing up as a ghoul and making fun of the horror movies he played.

We have a ROTTEN show for you today folks.

So, anyway, time marched on, I graduated from high school, and for a couple of years after that I drifted from job to college to job — looking for I don't know what.

Around then I got married, and we got a three-room apartment on 107th and Euclid, which was just about at the heart of things.

It was between two areas. One was the 105th and Euclid shopping area.
THEATER

In the 1930s, this had been the major shopping area in Cleveland outside of downtown.

Even when I moved there in 1959, it had five motion picture houses within a two-or three-block radius.
SHOCKING TALES
THE LOST CONTINENT
SHOCKING TALES

It used to be a classy shopping area, but now things were going bad. Some of the same old stores and restaurants that had been there for decades were still there, but they were on the verge of going bankrupt.

THE TASTY SHOP

In the '30s Jews were still plentiful around 105th and Euclid, but many had moved to the suburbs.

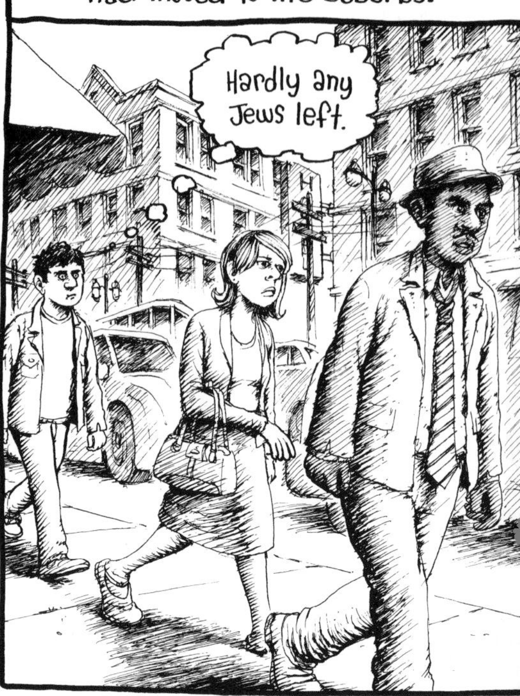
Hardly any Jews left.

Now it was a Skid Row area, wedged between two ghetto neighborhoods.

One thing that was pretty nice: there was still plenty of good live jazz to be heard.

But y'know, everybody hadn't left. There were still interesting guys hanging out, so there was a social life for me.

Now right up against 105th and Euclid was the University— Case Western.

As you'd expect, there were plenty of students there, who were fine to deal with, plus an excellent art museum, and Severance Hall, home of the World Famous Cleveland Orchestra.

SEVERANCE HALL

There were a lot more educational institutions there, like the art and music schools, and lots of open areas to walk around in. There was always something going on there. A classic old film showing or chamber music.

So because of the fact that 105th and Euclid was one of the liveliest parts of Cleveland, I stayed there for about twelve years.
La Dolce Vita

I used to live in a row house. In the evening, people would congregate there, and, weather permitting, we'd sit on the steps and talk about everything from sports to politics to art.

To prove the caliber of people that hung around there, Robert Crumb moved from Philadelphia to around the corner from me in 1962 and stayed 'til '66, working at the American Greeting Card company.

Crumb even found a wife in Cleveland. He couldn't find one in Philadelphia.

Not that everything was hunky-dory. There was a lot of crime in the area.

Shortly after I moved into my place, a student who was working at a pharmacy across the street was found murdered on the high school lawn.

And then there was the aforementioned Hough and Glenville riots in 1965 and 1967, which brought the National Guard into the area.

I stayed until 1972, but my huge record collection was driving me out of the house, so I moved out that year.

My wife and I found a real nice six-room apartment in an old but interesting suburb, Cleveland Heights, for only $115.00 a month.

By then, I had held a steady civil service job at the VA hospital, so I could easily afford it.

Actually, the job might've saved my life. I had worked for short stretches as a US civil servant when I was seventeen, and although pay was low, I liked the security and fringe benefits I got there.

Later, in the mid '60s, the federal government paid better wages. My file clerk job at the VA hospital was so easy it required almost no thinking. I did my work while I had conversations with other employees and patients. My performance was still good enough, however, to win me special awards.

What more could I ask for? I had the best flunky job in the world.

In 1972, after I started writing comics, I used a lot of characters I'd met at the VA in my stories. There was Toby, the self-proclaimed "Genuine Nerd," who was a bright guy but said and did strange things. Later, it occured to me that he was autistic; he sometimes astounded people with his remarks.

White Castle hamburgers are at the top of the nerd food chain.

After a while they transferred him from a file clerk's job to driving a van. He liked that better; there were less distractions. When I got on the David Letterman show, I was able to get him on MTV and in some locally made films. He loved the recognition.

In my opinion this is OK, an average McDonald's hamburger.

Then there was Mr. Boats, a lively and intelligent black man, whose job involved transporting patients from their rooms to the X-ray department and back. He had a sly sense of humor and was always talking about how he hated R&B and rock'n'roll. He was a classical violinist.

That's all these kids care about is the beat, **THE BEAT!**

He wanted me to find him Nat "King" Cole records. I had built up a side business selling LPs I got for free or cheap to acquaintances.

NAT KING COLE

He owned a farm and, to my Knowledge, is still working it.

Emil Heifetz, a short VA patient, was a Jewish Alter Kocker. He thought he was the most entitled person in the world. When he came to the VA, all the Jewish doctors would hide before he'd ask them favors and "hock a chainik" (bug them).

Excuse me doctor.

A good storyteller with a great sense of humor, Emil would burst into song at the drop of a hat.

♫ Havah Nagilah ♫

Although born in Canada, he spoke good Yiddish. He knew my relatives and used to insult them, but I didn't argue with him.

Your uncle Harry with his bulging frog eyes...*

* Harry actually did look something like a frog.

I was divorced in 1972, and there were tons of pretty, reasonably intelligent young girls around, but I rarely had a date.

Mostly I think it's because they couldn't figure out where I was coming from. Plus I really wasn't interested in most of them except for sex, and they probably figured that out.

So, actually, what I was doing was hanging out all night on the corner, bull-shitting with my friends. But at least I had a good neighborhood to do it in. It was called Coventry, and it was the hippest place in the Cleveland area.

It's funny. A few years earlier, newspapers were writing articles about Coventry turning into the first suburban slum.
Allen Salon

But a bunch of housing must've developed in the University area, because now a bunch of students and young doctors were moving into Coventry.

Just like that, the neighborhood solidified. There wasn't any political pecking order, but when some collective work needed doing, people would show up to do it. Like they built a playground themselves.

Kids just out of high school, often Bohemians, used to live in or frequent the neighborhood. The first gourmet coffee house was set up in Coventry.

There were specialist tradesman working there, like silversmiths.

In the summer, on Sundays, the streets were crowded, but everyone kept their cool.

And we also had huge street fairs there. Tens of thousands of people from all over Cleveland would show up.

The crowds got so large that the powers-that-be broke up the fairs into spread-out, single-night events.

STREET FAIR
AUGUST 5th
6PM-10PM
food • Drinks
arts & crafts
Live Music
fun for kids & adults!

There was this one guy I watched for at the fairs who sold wind-up flying airplanes.

I got such a kick out of his rap that I featured it in a comic book story.

There was also a big neighborhood garden set up in a vacant lot. I knew a guy who used to live next door to it. He'd let people water their plants from his house.

Oh yeah, and we had midnight movies on Saturday nights. We must've been among the first cities to do this.
COVENTRY CINEMA
ROCKY HORROR
PICTURE SHOW
CANDIES

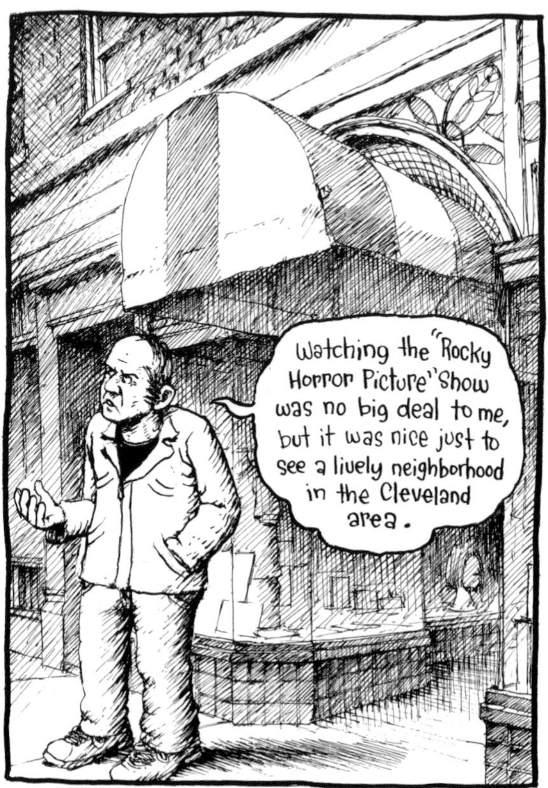
Watching the "Rocky Horror Picture" Show was no big deal to me, but it was nice just to see a lively neighborhood in the Cleveland area.

Music? Yeah there was plenty in several clubs. The kids were crazy about rock. Again, I was more into jazz, but it did my heart good just to see kids in clubs or swarming in the neighborhood's two excellent music stores.

We have a good used bookstore, too. The co-owner, Sue D'agatano, really promoted local writers with signings and readings. We had a nice poetry scene going on for a while.

Coventry is still a nice place to live, but it's not the attraction it once was.

The inner-ring suburbs like Cleveland Heights don't have the appeal they once did. The city's population is fairly well-divided between whites and blacks, but black kids are way overrepresented in the public school system.
ROLLING STONES

White families live in Cleveland Heights, for a little bit, but then move to outlying suburbs. When their kids get to school-age, some whites don't even consider moving into Cleveland Heights; they think it's down the tubes already!

This is a shame, because the Cleveland Heights Board of Education is leaving no stone unturned in its efforts to upgrade the schools!
GUEST AUTHORS

Cleveland Heights is still a quiet, law-abiding area. But it's been put "BEYOND THE PALE" by many whites!

And, of course, tax losses as a result of the recent recession haven't helped much either...

It is at times like this that I shifted my attention from my neighborhood to John Zubal's thriving book empire, which remained important to me.

John went to Fordham University in New York. There, he met and married Marilyn, a major catch, and moved back to Cleveland.

He took some graduate school classes, which left him with all but his dissertation to get a Ph.D. in History.

Meanwhile, he was teaching at a two-year Cleveland college and continuing to build his stock of books.

At first, he stored his books in other peoples' garages, among other places.

COOK BOOKS
AMERICAN HISTORY

His wife drew the line at their bedroom, however.

Don't you dare bring those in here.

Time went on, and finally he retired with a pension after twenty years of teaching.

Then he was able to turn his full attention to the book business, acquiring the three buildings on West 25th St. to display his wares.

ROMAN EMPIRE

John's rise has been steady since then, showing that it's possible in practice as well as theory to make money in Cleveland. We'll join him later.

I'd gotten divorced in 1972, and, aside from a date here and there, had had a pretty quiet love life. My isolation was really bugging me.

But in '77 things changed. A buddy of mine fixed me up with a girl, Jane Doe, who was a Ph.D. candidate in American Studies at Case Western.

She was bright, eager to learn, and nice-looking. She came over to my house for our first meeting, and we talked for hours. We had a lot in common, including quite an interest in politics, history, and literature.

After a while, I started getting nervous, though. I was successful, up to a point, in not putting my foot in my mouth. She wouldn't go home, so the next thing to do was try to get in bed with her. But I didn't want to risk making a pass at her and get shot down that night. I wanted to go to sleep alone and relish my good behavior.

Why doesn't she leave while things are going good!

So, finally, I had to make a pass at her, even though I was sleepy.

I was real nervous, having gone without sex for so long. I thought I'd screw up.

But for some strange reason, we clicked right off the bat. Boy, was I happy I'd dodged that bullet.

We stayed in bed all night and part of the next morning. I went to work, then met her at her place.

HI.

My luck held. Again I performed very well.

Now I'm not saying I'm some kinda stud, but there was some real good chemistry going on. After a while, I got real confident, and that's half the battle —more than half for me.

So we saw each other every day, went to all kinds of stuff, movies, even lectures.

I really liked the lectures. I was interested, as I said, in her work and wanted to learn more about it. That was a happy situation — I thought.

So after about six weeks of, for me, bliss, I was totally smitten, but I had always assumed that after she got her Ph.D. she'd be leaving Cleveland. So I was psychologically prepared for her departure.

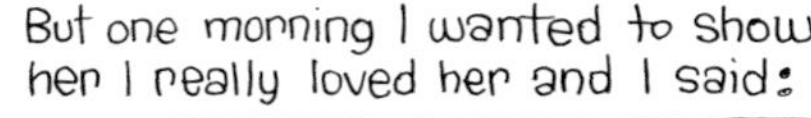
But one morning I wanted to show her I really loved her and I said:

You know, if I thought you were gonna stay around here after you graduated, I could get very serious about you.*
Toasted oats

* My job situation was so good and solid that I'd never leave it. It took years to set it up.

SHE said...
Well, I CAN be influenced.

You can be influenced? what does THAT mean!?
Toasted oats

Are you saying, if I marry you, you'll stay in Cleveland and try to make it here?
Yes.
Toasted oats

WOW, UNBELIEVABLE! Let's go get a LICENSE!
Toasted oats

Actually, it **WAS** unbelievable, but after the grim years I'd spent between 1959 and 1977, I figured I had nothing to lose. I was right about that, too!

I thought, though, that at least some woman out there would be interested in hooking up with someone who had so much in common with her intellectually. I mean anything is possible.

And I already knew more about some aspects of her studies than she did. Like she had, what was to me, an an amazing ignorance of history.

NO, that happened about ten years after that!

But that year we had a wonderful summer. Remember, I told you that even though Cleveland was in decline there were still plenty of things we could do together. Remember what I said about museums and parks.

We even went on a really nice picnic with her classmates in a Case Western Reserve rural property called "the Pink Pig."
Wow, this is the life.

If she dumps me tomorrow, it will have still been worth it.

But I still thought she might leave me after she got her degree and had to face the cold world.

God, I hope she stays.

We both knew that Cleveland wasn't the best place for an ambitious Ph.D. academic to live. Even at its best, Cleveland has never been known as a center for the study of humanities.

Plus, she badly wanted to teach at a prestigious university, preferably in the Ivy League. The only prestigious college in the Cleveland area, Oberlin, turned her down.

Didn't get it, huh?

Gradually, things started to cool with us. For one, she didn't want to go to lectures with me anymore.

That's ok, I'll go by myself.

She never told me exactly why, but I think it had to do with my lowly social status.

To her I'm getting to be a bum!

At that time, I was getting flattering reviews from not only trade publications but more prestigious publications like the Village Voice.

WOW, look at this! This is a really nice write-up!
VILLAGE
VOICE

But I was losing money on the comic book, and nobody, aside from comics fans and insiders, knew about me.

Everybody's into SUPERHEROES!

In 1980, I did get a call from Jonathan Demme about him making a film based on "American Splendor," but he wasn't well-known either and the deal went nowhere.

My wife would go out for long periods during the day and refused to tell me where she'd been.

I started to realize my fear would come true, that once she had her degree she'd view me as a liability and **DUMP** me!

I had made another wrong guess about her. I didn't realize what an upwardly mobile person she wanted to be.

See, it wouldn't be too much of a problem for her to get a job at a so-so local college or university.

Sure there wouldn't be any prestige connected to that, but the main way academics get prestige is publishing articles, and you don't have to be from an Ivy League school to publish articles.

She could've stayed in Cleveland, which she kind of liked, and gotten articles published, which, if well-received, would have boosted her national status as an academic.

Actually, she did get a job working at a local Catholic girls' college, but she regarded it as a stopgap, and quit after a year.

URSULINE
COLLEGE

Furthermore, I didn't see her doing much serious work on getting an article together during that time.

She Could be writing something right now!

So y'know, now I'm in a position of waiting for the axe to drop.
One evening she said:
Harvey, I think I'm going to move out of town...
And I don't want you coming with me.
What's up? What'd I do?
Nothing— I just don't think I can get the position I want here.
Well, I'm not about to follow you out of town, you don't have to worry about that! I got a setup that really suits me here. If you think I'm gonna give up the decent life I've set up in Cleveland to follow your path to possible Ivy League stardom, you're 100% WRONG!

So then she goes in to bed. I get a blanket and lay down on the couch.
I'm fixing to sleep out **HERE!**

After a while she comes out of the bedroom and says:

Harvey, aren't you gonna come to bed with me?

C'mon, don't be stubborn.

Wow, she expected me to sleep with her after she dumps me. I dunno... I guess we were living in two different worlds.

What is she, crazy?!

Moreover, she comes out of the bed-room a few more times, trying to get me in like it was business as usual.

Changed your mind yet?

Well, we went to a marriage counselor, more as a matter of form than anything else. She wasn't gonna change her mind.

So I split the money in the bank account 50-50 with her, even though I couldn't recall her putting in anything.

That allowed her to live in Cleveland for months while she looked for a proper job all over the place.

NEW YORK TIMES
CLASSIFIEDS

I had fallen from avant-garde comic book writer to schlep file clerk.

I guess it all depends on the angle you're looking at me from. Anyway, we officially broke up in February 1982, after 3½ years. It was OK, though. At least I had some fun in the beginning.

It could have been worse.

She eventually got a job at a small college in New England. It wasn't an Ivy League college, but it seemed that New England was close enough.

I also bought her car for twice as much as she paid for it. I hadn't owned a car since 1960, but I got used to sharing one with her.

So it was a pretty easy separation. I'd sort of realized its possibility from day one and, when it was over, became resigned to it pretty quickly.

I'll be OK.

What happened to her? Well, she took a job at a New England school, where she thought she was on a tenure track.

But it turned out she wasn't, so she put plan B into effect.

Her brother-in-law had hooked her up with a lawyer, so she married him, had a couple of kids, and, from what I heard, was leading a pretty comfortable life as a suburban housewife.

She didn't completely give up on academia, however. Several years ago, she had a book published about this guy she'd been real interested in as a student.

Once, when I was going to a talk at Brown University, her daughter, who was going there, came up and introduced herself to me.

I was pretty surprised, and we didn't have much to say to each other.

You know, it went out with a whimper, not a bang.

So anyway, after I got divorced again (I got dumped by wife #1 in 1972), I was scared because the first two times I'd been divorced I'd gone months without a date afterward.

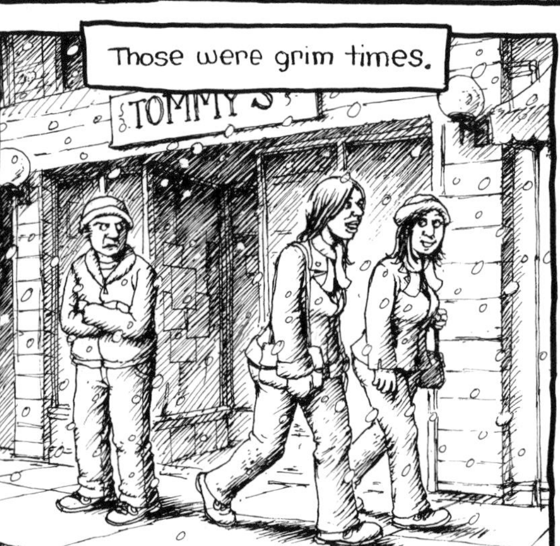
Those were grim times.
TOMMY'S

But this time it wasn't so bad. I got fixed up with a nurse, and we hung out with each other for several months.

Then I started corresponding with a woman who ran a comic book shop and worked for the State Prison system in Delaware.

AMERICAN SPLENDOR

$1.00

$2.00

We started writing each other in August, and telephoning each other in December.

We finally met in February of 1983 and decided to get married in May in Wilmington. The Mayor married us.

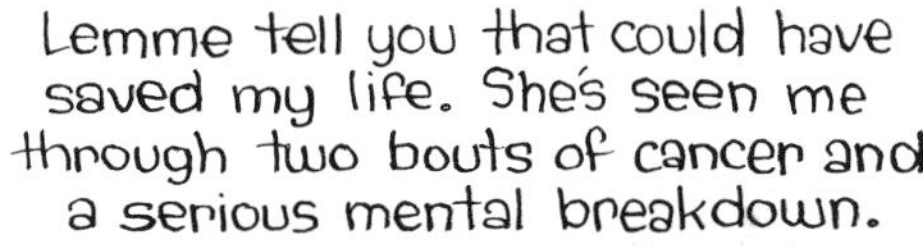
Lemme tell you that could have saved my life. She's seen me through two bouts of cancer and a serious mental breakdown.

Plus she helped me further my career as a comic book writer (she's a fine one herself).

Well, we've written about some of the stuff we've done together elsewhere, but if you haven't read about it in books like, "Our Cancer Year," I'm updating you now.

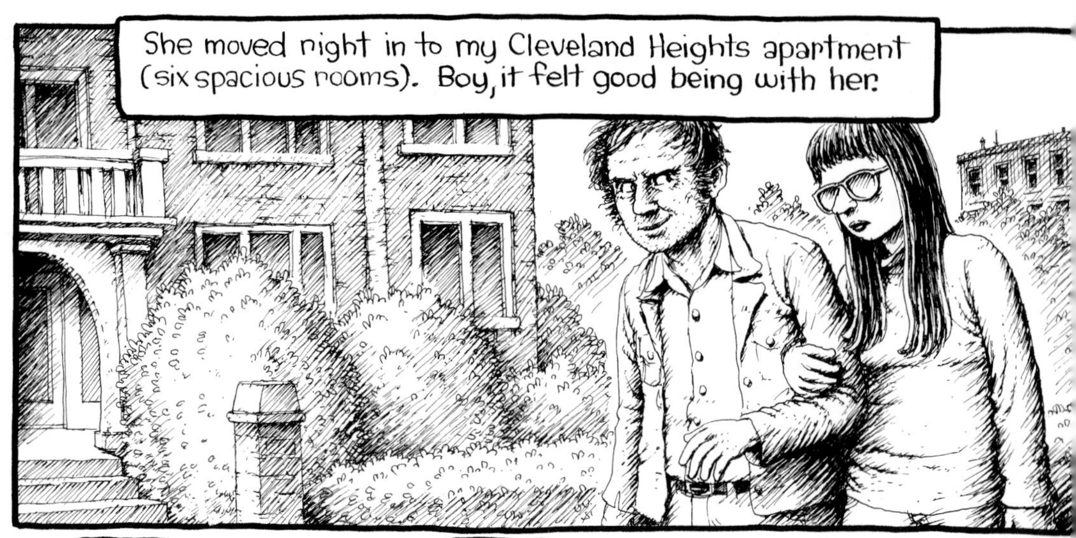
She moved right in to my Cleveland Heights apartment (six spacious rooms). Boy, it felt good being with her.

So now I had my excellent (for me) VA gig, a great wife, and a nice apartment in a great neighborhood.

Plus my comics writing career started to pick up steam. How lucky can a guy get?

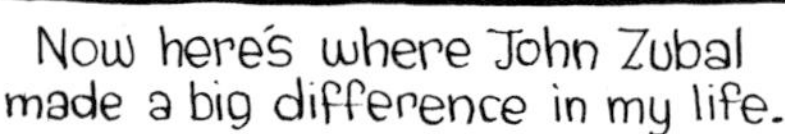
Now here's where John Zubal made a big difference in my life.

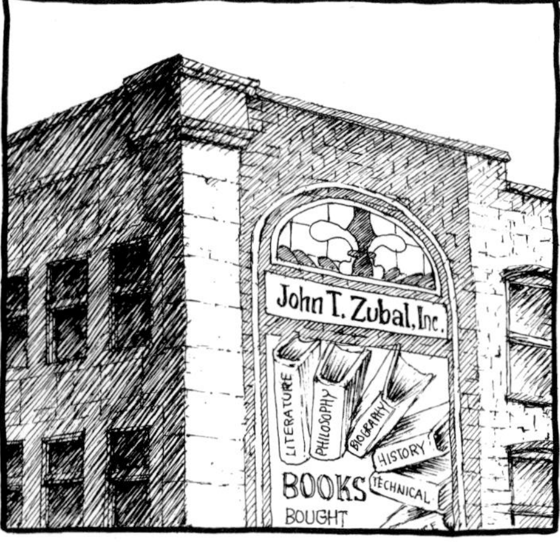
John T. Zubal, Inc.
LITERATURE
PHILOSOPHY
BIOGRAPHY
HISTORY
TECHNICAL
BOOKS
BOUGHT

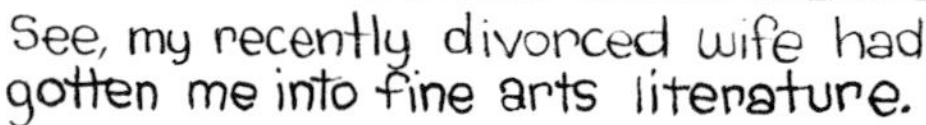
See, my recently divorced wife had gotten me into fine arts literature.

I mean, I'd read plenty of good fiction before, but now I decided I would show her a thing or two. I'd learn more about literature than she knew.

I'll beat her at her own game!

Man, I worked it like a madman, enjoying it as I read. It was a pleasure, not a chore. I loved the stuff.

First I'd read the literary histories of certain geographical regions in different eras, then I'd get what were supposed to be the major books written there, and then read them critically.

Then I'd write articles about the authors in these little magazines, like I did with jazz criticism.

It was great. I discovered some outstanding writers who'd been forgotten, and some who I thought were overrated.

God this George Ade is good. He was popular once, but he's been forgotten.

Now, I'll say one thing about Cleveland, they have a lot of library sales there. You can pick up some rare books for $.50 or $1.00. There was something going on almost every weekend.

BOOK SALE

So I bought tons of stuff for myself, but I also got books to trade.
CHECK OUT

If I found clean first editions with dust jackets on them, I'd bring them to John.
AL INC.
JOHN T. ZOBAL
BOOKS BOUGHT & SOLD

He had a lot of rare books that I wanted that didn't have dust jackets or weren't first editions, and he'd trade them to me because he could get little or no money from them.
OK, we got a deal.

He was very generous, too.
Here, take this one along with you; I can't do much with it.

Hoping to reciprocate, I tried to get him publicity.

Hey John, there's this guy named Anthony Bourdain who wants me on his national TV show. He collects books. So I told him about you, and he wants to do a segment of his show about Zubals.

One of the buildings he owned had formerly, as I said, been a Hostess Bakery, and it still had pipes running through it that contained the stuff they put in Twinkies. It had been there 10 or 15 years, but the stuff was all chemicals and didn't rot after all that time.

It was still edible, and Bourdain tasted it on the show.

It's Twinki-licious.

Boy, that was a day to remember. Anthony Bourdain loved the huge collection of cookbooks John had, especially since he was a chef.

where'd you get this? I never knew such a book existed.

But, by that time, I myself was not the avid collector of books and records I used to be.

My record collection had started when I was 16. I became a jazz fanatic, and for decades was a jazz critic for various publications. I had a hard time letting go of any record.

Y'never know when this might come in handy.

At the same time, for reasons connected partly with getting even with my second wife, I had begun building this huge book collection, and was writing literary criticism.

My collections grew so large that they were a major factor in me buying a house.

FOR SALE

But even the house wasn't big enough to house the amount of stuff I'd accumulated.

My wife was increasingly annoyed with this, especially when I virtually stopped writing music and literary pieces.

What use do you have for all this? It's strangling us!
Ulp

When are we going to get rid of it?
I know, I know, but a lot is valuable. We gotta figure out how t' get some money out of it!

Lemme think about it a few days.

And days stretch into weeks and weeks into months and years. I'm gonna get rid of them!

So, eventually, my wife searched the Internet looking for a store to sell the LPs and CDs.

Finally...
Well, I think I know where we can get the best deal on your music stuff.
ULP

She got a hold of a used record store in New Jersey. They would come to Cleveland in a truck to pick it up.

Then, one day, a truck from there pulled up with a couple of guys.

They're here. I can't bear to watch them load up.

In about half a day, the heart of my jazz collection was gone.

At least I still have my books.

That's what I thought.
I gave a bunch of your Russian books to a friend of mine.

OH NO! God, I LOVE modern Russian literature!

It'll take YEARS to replace them. It's not worth it.
Good. I was hoping you'd reach that conclusion.

I was left with just PART of my book collection.

But a part of a collection, after all the years I'd put into accumulating the stuff, is NOTHING, no collection at all.

So, for a while, I walked around kinda stunned. But I got used to it.
I feel better today.

I mean, it was for the best. I was burned out on writing music and literary criticism anyway.

I seldom read or listen to stuff these days. I mostly just lay around listening to NPR.
This is Neal Conan with "Talk of the Nation."

I'm not the voracious seeker of knowledge I used to be...

Although I sure don't regret the time I spent putting in to it.

The stuff I used to read about helps me write historical, political, and biographical as well as auto-biographical "graphic novels."

Yeah, I write as much as I can; I have to make a living. I made a big mis-calculation when I thought that my pension and Social Security money would take care of my expenses.

They don't even come close.

I still have a basic knowledge of several subjects, and I go back to them and write about them when possible.

It's still fun for me to review material that I dealt with years ago.

Cleveland's been in decline for years, as many of you know. Recently, a study showed that it was losing inhabitants faster than any of the major population centers.
90
Hwy
Downtown
Cleveland

But I'm not gonna worry about that too much. My neighborhood is still pretty pleasant.
CLEVELAND
HEIGHTS
WELCOMES YOU

Anytime I want, I take a nice walk.

The last couple of winters haven't been too bad, either. Maybe because of global warming.

Y'now, it's funny for me now. I look in the mirror and see I've lost a lotta hair. So I realize I'm getting old.

I mean, I'm seventy. That's way on the downslope.

But still, I don't feel all creaky and stuff. Who knows? Maybe I'll keep going for a while.

I mean, there have been times when things looked pretty bleak for me.
Like all the important stuff in my life had already taken place.

But y'know, I really don't wanna give in to that. If you're gonna be alive, you oughta at least make an effort to feel good.

I've got a few good friends left, though. Like there's my buddy, Lee. He's a college graduate, but he's pretty much had a hard time getting a good job.

He's had a wide range of janitorial gigs. Once, he was a janitor at the local movie theatre.
SODA
LEE

That startled me, because he was well-educated and articulate. Why couldn't he find a better gig?

Like, look at me. I don't have a college degree, but I had a civil service job that suited me fine. I bet he'd like it too.

He's been a newspaper reporter, an environmental activist with the Sierra Club, and stuff, but he hasn't been able to get better jobs.

Now Lee is working the second shift at a local copy shop.

How many copies did you need?
LEE

But he's also studying to be an occupational therapy assistant at a two-year college. It's great that he's still ambitious.

He's got a real good relationship with my wife. She hooks him up with places that give him cheap dental and medical work.

And he helps her do work around the house. He's a real good handyman. On the other hand, I can't fix or clean anything good, no matter how hard I try.

He's been hanging out in neighborhoods I've lived in for years. We have a lot of mutual acquaintances.

tommy's

FEDERAL RESERVE
He's full of good stories about them, and about local politics.

He picked up a lot of stuff when he was a reporter and activist.

They didn't want this freeway built but...

As a matter of fact, I've been thinking of writing a book with him, or hooking him up with someone that'd publish his own book.

I get a pleasure from setting up people with stuff like jobs, acting as a go-between.

I'd like ya to meet one of my oldest and dearest friends.

It makes me feel like a mover and shaker.
EBEE

Although, overall, I've been letting friendly relationships with people drift.

That's not good. The older ya get, the more of a social life ya need. At least I do, even though I lay around way too much.

I've worked out a routine, so that I at least don't feel like I'm wasting all my retired time.

I get up at 6:30, feed my cats, take a bath, get dressed, and then go out and water the plants.

I never cared much about keeping the lawn looking nice, but my wife has lately gotten into gardening, and I feel like I should do a little to help.

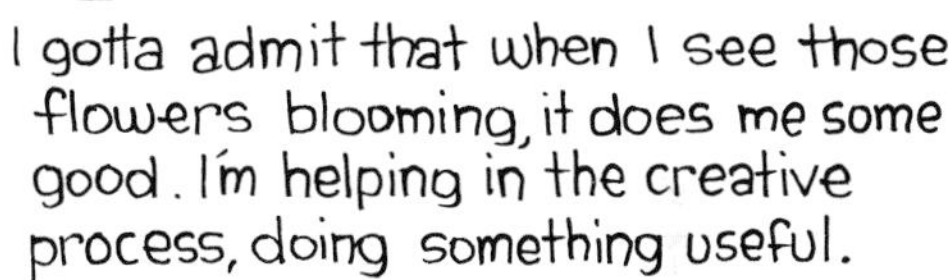
I gotta admit that when I see those flowers blooming, it does me some good. I'm helping in the creative process, doing something useful.

I especially dig watching the tomatoes grow. I mean, I like tomatoes, and to be able to pick 'em off the vine–that satisfies.

I wish we grew more vegetables. Cucumbers, bell peppers, leaf lettuce – those are among my favorites.

But my wife has chosen herbs, spices, and flowers. I don't mix in because it's her project, and I do get something out of it, so why cause a commotion?

well, it's what she wants.

Maybe next year there'll be more vegetables – onions that I can put on cheese and tomato sandwiches, potatoes that I can fry.

Yeah, or corn. Man, wouldn't I love to bust off an ear of corn, go into the house, boil it, and sprinkle some salt and butter on it? That'd make me feel like Orville Redenbacher.

Who knows what surprises await me?
RENAISSANCE HOTEL

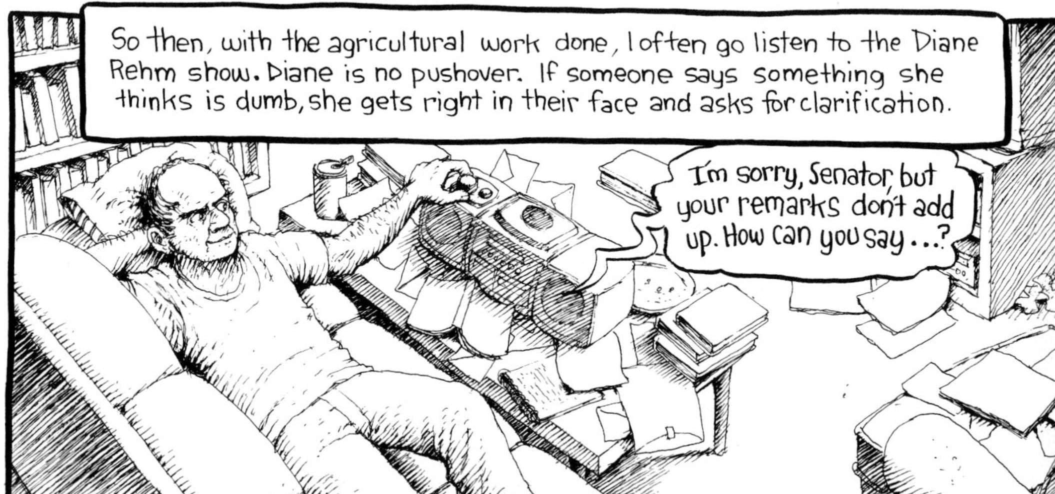
So then, with the agricultural work done, I often go listen to the Diane Rehm show. Diane is no pushover. If someone says something she thinks is dumb, she gets right in their face and asks for clarification.
I'm sorry, Senator, but your remarks don't add up. How can you say...?

And, man, even though she was 72 the last time I heard, she's still very attractive. Somebody pulled my coat to that.

She's drop dead beautiful.

Wanna see her picture on the Internet?
Yeah, sure, if you've got the time.

You're right, she is very nice looking.

Now that I'm up in age myself, I really root for people in their seventies.

Also, in the morning, I try to work on various writing projects.

Right now I'm doing a book on how I changed my mind about Israel, a survey of Yiddish fiction writing, the piece I'm working on about Cleveland, and an article about guitarist Shawn Lane.

CLEVELAND

The guy who wants me to do the Lane piece is going to use it for some kind of introduction to a project. Lane wasn't well-known, but he was a fantastic player. I'm happy to write about him.

I'm also gonna try t'do a history of jazz, and have a book published on the rise of and conflict between liberalism and conservatism in the USA.

See, even though I don't have the pure intellectual interest in learning that I once had, making a living involves keeping my nose in a book.

It's good that I have that drive, because, even though I'm not as passionate about learning as I was, it's still often stimulating.

Well, after I get through writing and studying, what do I do in Cleveland?

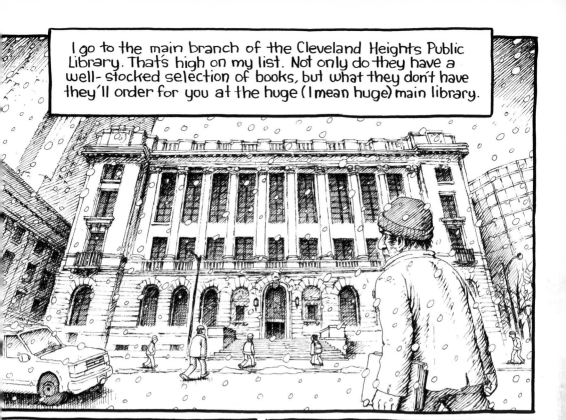

I go to the main branch of the Cleveland Heights Public Library. That's high on my list. Not only do they have a well-stocked selection of books, but what they don't have they'll order for you at the huge (I mean huge) main library.

The Cleveland Public Library has got to be one of the greatest libraries in America. It was built in n era when Cleveland businessmen had plenty of money and were willing to spend it on the public.

I was told when I was a kid that the main branch of the Cleveland Public Library had more books in it than any library building but the main one in New York.

It's amazing what they have – everything from English to Yiddish books.

Ah, I finally ran down a copy of this.

If you're a scholar, you should have access to good libraries, and in Cleveland you're all set.
PALMS

Between Zubal's and the Cleveland-area libraries, you can look up anything.
LAKE LAND

Other than that, I can't think of any place I hang out at regularly, except for my post office box, waiting for letters that praise me.

Praise is very hard to come by in Cleveland. People here are bitter; I can't blame 'em. I still haven't gotten over how we lost the 1954 World Series.

People come to my house sometimes to meet me or get an autograph.

Hi Harvey, I just got in from Michigan and came right over. Sorry I didn't call first, but it's ok right?

See, my number and address are in the phone book. It makes it easier for fans to come by and praise me.

But seriously, folks, the meetings are genuinely enjoyable. So far, no one's come over to throw a pie in my face.

I'm not connected to the comic book community and seldom hear from anyone in it. So when people come over who dig my work, I feel less isolated.
Lemme buy you a cuppa coffee.

I really like it when they say they like my complaining because they have the same problems I do, and it's nice to know they're not alone in this world.
Yeah I had an experience like that.

My girlfriend hates me.
Don't take it so hard. There's probably something wrong with her.

After I hear some of these people, I feel like it's nice to know I'm not alone in this world, either.

It's astonishing how much some of them know about my work.
In that story you did in #10...
Hold on, is that the one with the dish-washing cover?

It's great that many of them aren't as neurotic as I am.
So you're in advertising, but you'd like to get into comics?

well, first of all, it's fine to have the energy to take on a lot of work, but don't quit your day job.

Even if you're a terrific author/cartoonist, there's no guarantee anyone will publish your work.

And even if they do, chances are they'll pay you little or nothing for your work. To a lot of people, publishing comics is a labor of love.

They lose money themselves.
Uh-huh.

I mean, if you really enjoy doing comics, and you think you're creative, by all means keep at it.
Oh sure, I like doin' them.

But it took thirty years and a movie based on my work to make me any money.

Not even being on the David Letterman show helped my sales. That's why I finally went ballistic on his program. It was calculated. Not only was he tryin' to restrict what I had to say, he wasn't makin' me any **BREAD**!

Everyone has their price, but I'm not gonna sell out for **NOTHIN**!

Another thing, you don't live in a media center. If you live in a media center, you have a huge advantage.
Is Denver a media center?

Nope. It's a pretty big city, but not a media center.

CHECKS
LEASE
Yep, I could write my own "Guide to the Perplexed."

I'd pick up where Maimonides left off.
LEASE
513-532-2554

Y'know, life ain't fair, and that's especially true in the arts.

My daily routine isn't very exciting. Like I said, I get up at 6:30 AM then go water the plants.

I eat my breakfast, usually graham crackers and milk in a bowl, or a honeybun (6 for $1.59) and a glass of milk. Thanks to a lot of milk, I'm not a total physical wreck yet.

I'm sort of Cleveland Heights' answer to the beloved literary character, Tevye the Milkman (from "Fiddler on the Roof").

I read The Cleveland Plain Dealer and The New York Times every day. I've been into political and economic matters for a long time.

It all started during the economic recession of 1959. I was wondering why I couldn't get a job. Being in Cleveland didn't help.

But these times are way tougher than in the late 1950's. There's no telling how bad they are going to get.

All those people who scrimped and saved for their retirement, and now their savings have been reduced in value by 35% to 50%.

Guess how much money I lost in the last few months.
I dunno.

A quarter to a half of what I had set aside for retirement.

Now I'm gonna have to work 'til I drop, and I'm one of the lucky ones; I still have a job—at least for the time being.
BAKERY
I like Obama a lot, but how's he gonna be able to spend the money he needs to get things back on track? Congress wants results, but doesn't want to pay for them.
Our deficit is ballooning.
We've gotta take CHANCES to turn this thing around!
SALE
216-398-4728
But look, Congress doesn't even want to approve a small tax increase on people who earn over $250,000 a year.
NOBODY in America wants to raise taxes now, no matter how little the increase is! It's like the government is voluntarily surrendering power. They're cutting off an arm!
Well, these days, Cleveland isn't the worst place for me to be. Now every-one's depressed, not just yours' truly!

I look around, I see homeless people and vacated buildings! **GOD**, I hope I can keep on eking out the bread!
LIQUOR
35

Yeah, the mood is somber in Cleveland, which is emptying out fast. What's gonna happen next?! How are they gonna solve the unemployment problem when businesses refuse to hire new people?

There's some talk about a medical mart, a sort of one-stop for medical supplies, which apparently doesn't exist anywhere in the world yet.

CLEVELAND MEDICAL MART &
CONVENTION CENTER

Some say it will bring a BONANZA to our city.

Wouldn't I love to see that.
LAUNDROMAT

ACME
END

A Pal's Goodbye

By Jimi Izrael

Much of Harvey Pekar's improbable life was very Cleveland, very Midwestern. He was a painfully ordinary guy. There are no celebrities on the streets of Cleveland. Not if they know what's good for them. Cleveland is one of the last places in America you can live and die as if you were never here, and no one will raise a glass to you, no matter who you are or what you did.

People don't come here to the Midwest to dream—they are here because it's cheap, and they stay because it's cheap, and in the likely event you lose your job filing papers, flipping burgers or breaking rocks, you won't have far to fall. You get lots of props for a good try, maybe more for a failure. More? Yeah, almost certainly. Someone will buy you a drink. But if you try hard enough to bring the eyes and accolades from afar, well—you'll never live it down. (Who told you to try so damn hard anyways?) Harvey was the secret treasure of a city struggling not to fall into the Lake. Harvey saw Cleveland as it is, looking from the bottom up. He wasn't interested in turning Cleveland into a hub of new culture or being the vanguard of a new literary movement. He loved writing, but he wasn't stylish or self-absorbed enough to qualify as a stereotypical artist or bohemian. Not trendy enough to be a hipster of today. This is a working man's town. So he worked, he hustled and read and wrote in the between time. And Harvey Pekar was one of America's finest writers. There are people who will tell you otherwise and dispute my assertion as the sentimental hyperbole of a fan, friend and aspiring academic. I don't know that you're wrong. This truth, though, is the same as with any great artist and his work: either you get Harvey, or you don't.

People say "Harvey Pekar was Cleveland," and they mean it as a backhanded compliment, at best. They mean the Harvey Pekar As Seen on TV, the file clerk immortalized on celluloid as twitchy, itchy, grumpy and unlikable. That's not the Harvey I knew—the guy who took me to work with him that summer in the early '90s to meet the people who populated the world he was writing about, so I could hear the texture of their voices and see them the way he heard them. This lesson was the most valuable as it turned out. For years, I could call him for writing tips or marital advice. He was there for me. I stopped by his house just a week or so before he passed, and he was the same Harvey—we kvetched about the life of a writer in a shithole like Cleveland before I shook his hand and made my way to the Food Co-op. Harvey was the sweet, kindly Jewish grandfather I never had. And I miss him dearly.

But not for nothing, I get the other thing, too.

Cleveland's a tough, slightly bowed, achy, gray, crotchety, charitable town with moments of brilliance and unexpected, often ironic laughter. Like Harvey. So yeah. I get that.

Jimi Izrael
Cleveland
August 25th, 2011

Jimi Izrael is a writer and journalist from East Cleveland, Ohio. He teaches a class called "*American Splendor: The Comic Book Chronicles of Cleveland's Harvey Pekar*" for Case Western Reserve University's SAGES Program. He is the Harvey Pekar Scholar. Because Joyce said so, and you don't argue with Joyce if you know what's good for you.

Thank You

Joyce Brabner, *SMITH Magazine*, Dean Haspiel, Sean Pryor, Rick Parker, Seth Kushner, Jonathan Vankin, Alan Moore, Paul Gravett, Melinda Gebbie, Brian Heater, Lisa Ullmann, Chris Staros, Jay Babcock, Heidi MacDonald, Calvin Reid, Jackie Estrada, Michele Reznik, Chandler Moses, Jay Lynch, Kim Deitch, Jimi Izrael, Josh Neufeld, Josh Bernstein, Toby Radloff, and Josh Frankel.

Photo by Brian Heater/*The Daily Cross Hatch*

A happy Harvey at his 70th birthday party/ *Pekar Project* gallery show at Pennello Gallery in Cleveland.

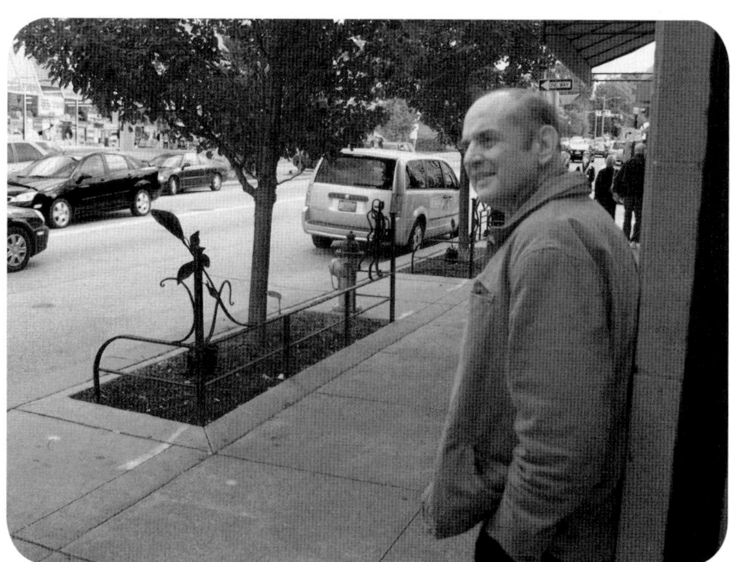

Photo by Brian Heater/*The Daily Cross Hatch*

Harvey on his home turf, hangin' in Coventry.

Photo by Seth Kushner

Harvey Pekar (October 8, 1939–July 12, 2010) was born in Cleveland, Ohio, his home all his life. In 1959 Pekar began writing for *The Jazz Review* and ultimately wrote hundreds of articles and reviews. He landed a job as a file clerk at a VA Hospital in 1965, held until retirement in 2001. He started writing autobiographical comics in 1972. The first collected edition of his *American Splendor* comics won the American Book Award in 1987. In 1994, the graphic novel *Our Cancer Year* (co-written with his wife, Joyce Brabner) won the Harvey Award.

An *American Splendor* film featuring Paul Giamatti as Pekar was released in 2003, winning awards at Sundance and Cannes. 2005 saw the release of *The Quitter*, a graphic novel about his early years, illustrated by Dean Haspiel. In 2009, he began creating webcomics for *SMITH Magazine*'s PEKAR PROJECT which you can read at www.smithmag.net/pekarproject.

Photo by Seth Kushner

Joseph Remnant is a Los Angeles-based artist, who previously illustrated Harvey Pekar stories for *SMITH Magazine*'s PEKAR PROJECT. His comics and illustrations have appeared in *Arthur Magazine*, *Juxtapoz*, and *The New York Times*. He recently self-published the first issue of his own comic titled "BLINDSPOT." More art and info at josephremnant.com.